"Eloi Eloi, lama sabachthani?"
[My God, my God, why have you forsaken me?]
—Mark 15:34, NIV

©1997-2003 Troy Nilsson
©2005 Standard Publishing, Cincinnati, Ohio
A division of Standex International Corporation
refuge™ is a trademark of Standard Publishing
EMPOWERED® Youth Products is a trademark of Standard Publishing
All rights reserved. Printed in China.

Project editor: Dale Reeves
Cover and interior design: Scott Ryan
Cover art ©1997 Troy Nilsson
Special thanks to Tabitha Neuenschwander, the journaling diva

Scripture quotations marked NLT are taken from the Holy Bible, NEW LIVING TRANSLATION, copyright © 1996. Used by permission of Tyndale House Publishers, Inc., Wheaton, Illinois 60189. All rights reserved.
Scripture quotations marked NIV are taken from the HOLY BIBLE, NEW INTERNATIONAL VERSION®. NIV®. Copyright © 1973, 1978, 1984 by International Bible Society. Used by permission of Zondervan. All rights reserved.
Scripture quotations marked THE MESSAGE are taken from THE MESSAGE, copyright © by Eugene H. Peterson, 1993, 1994, 1995. Used by permission of NavPress Publishing Group.

12 11 10 09 08 07 06 05
7   6   5   4   3   2   1

ISBN 0-7847-1659-5

refuge™ journals

Standard Publishing
Cincinnati, Ohio

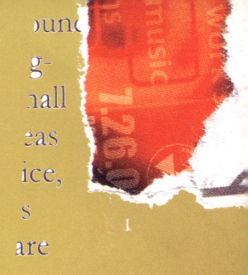

"Forgiving the unforgivable is hard. So was the cross: hard words, hard wood, hard nails."

—William S. Stoddard

"If you love your enemies you w
love is the power of redemptio
—Martin Luther King, Jr.

iscover that at the very root of

"It was a perfect sacrifice by a perfect person to perfect some very imperfect people."

—Hebrews 10:14, THE MESSAGE

"My life is poured out like water,
   and all my bones are out of joint.
My heart is like wax,
   melting within me.
My strength has dried up like sunbaked clay.
   My tongue sticks to the roof of my mouth.
   You have laid me in the dust and left me
   for dead."

—Psalm 22:14, 15, NLT

"Christ is the Son of God. He died to atone for men's sin, and after three days rose again. This is the most important fact in the universe. I die believing in Christ."
—Watchman Nee,
note found under his pillow, in prison, at his death

"I tell you the truth,
today you will be with
me in paradise."
—Luke 23:43, NIV

"The blood of Jesus Christ has great power! There is perhaps not a phrase in the Bible that is so full of secret truth as is 'The blood of Jesus.' It is the secret of His incarnation, when Jesus took on flesh and blood; the secret of His obedience unto death, when He gave His life at the cross of Calvary; the secret of His love that went beyond all understanding when He bought us with His blood; the secret of the enemy and the secret of our eternal salvation."

—Corrie ten Boom

"Christ has not only spoken to us by his life but has also spoken for us by his death."
—Søren Kierkegaard

"A God who has nothing to do with our laughing and our weeping, our fear or our boredom, a God who is absolutely 'beyond' all human experience—such a God would have absolutely no meaning for us."
—anonymous

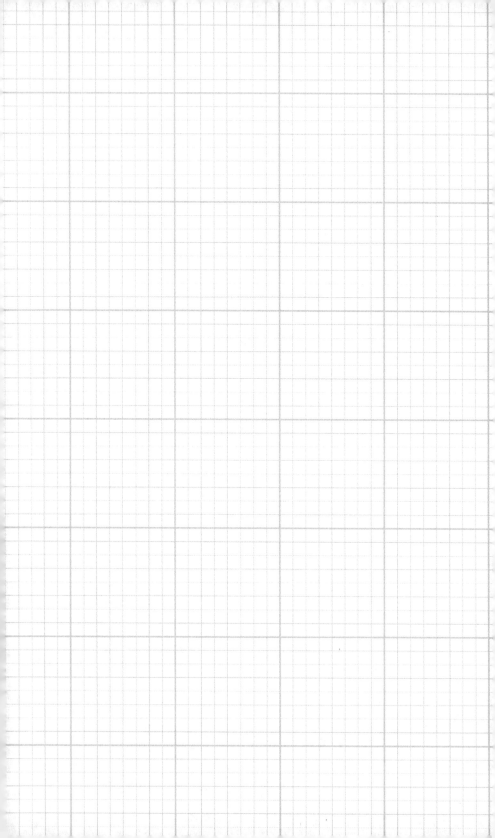

"I am ready to die for my Lord, that in my blood the Church may obtain liberty and peace."

—Thomas à Becket,
Archbishop of Canterbury

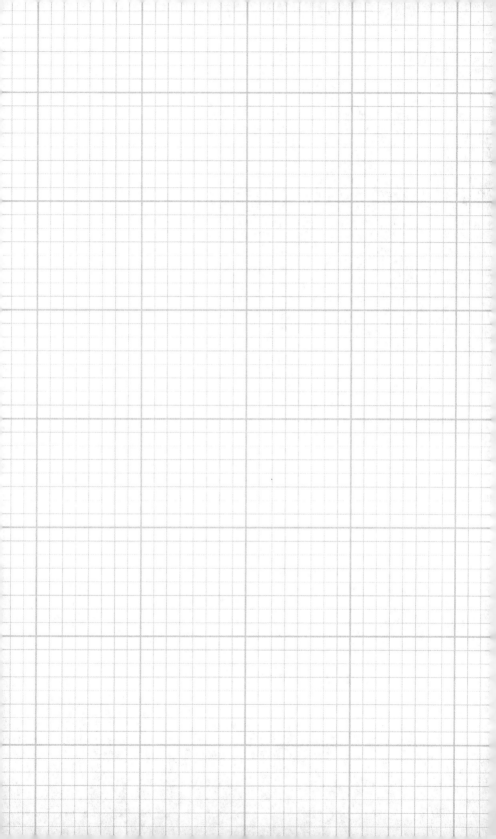

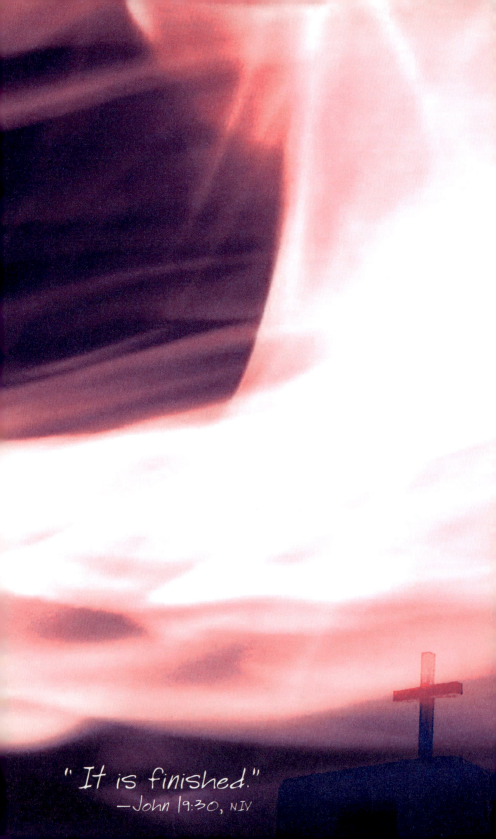

"Let it [crucifixion] never come near th[e] body of a Roman citizen; nay, not even nea[r] his thoughts, or eyes, or ears."
—Cicero, Roman historian

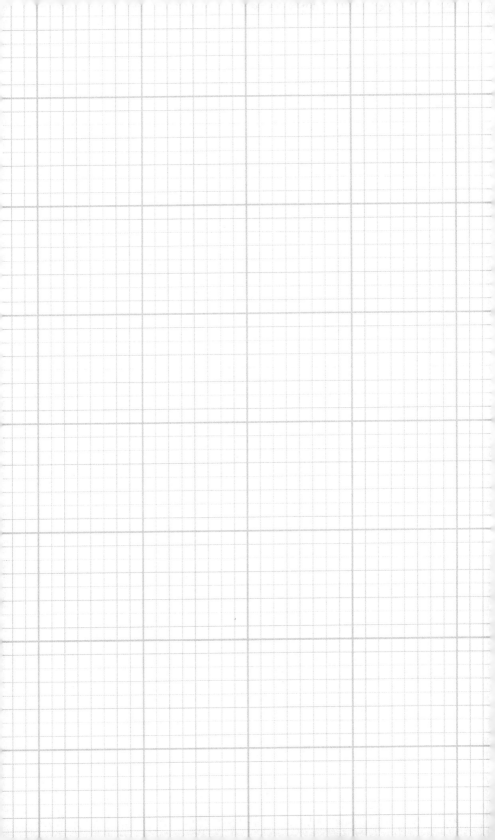

"...all the broken and dislocated pieces of the universe—people and things, animals and atoms—get properly fixed and fit together in vibrant harmonies, all because of his death, his blood that poured down from the Cross."
—Colossians 1:20, THE MESSAGE

"I am thirsty."
—John 19:28, NIV

"Take your pen once more and write cross it all: 'The blood of Jesus Christ His Son cleanses us from all sin!'"
—Martin Luther

"He was pierced for our transgressions,
    he was crushed for our iniquities;
the punishment that brought us peace was upon him,
    and by his wounds we are healed."

—Isaiah 53:5, NIV

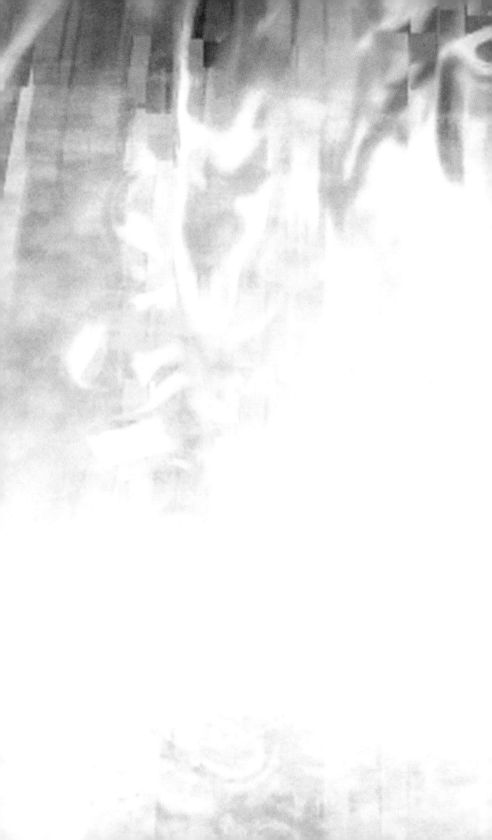

"Love is the Cross,
and the Cross is Love."
—St. Terese of The Child Jesus

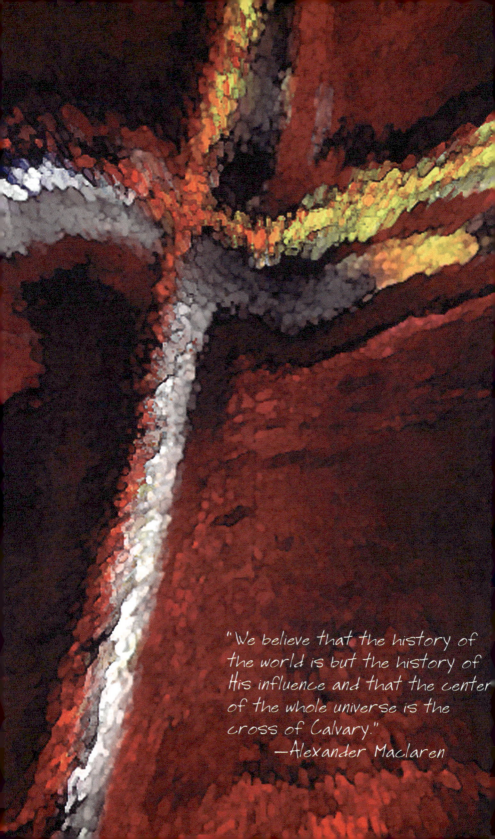

"Now that we are set right with God by means of this sacrificial death, the consummate blood sacrifice, there is no longer a question of being at odds with God in any way."
—Romans 5:9, THE MESSAGE

"It was not human beings who accomplished anything here; no, God alone did it. He came to human beings in infinite love. He judged what is human. And he granted grace beyond any merit."
—Dietrich Bonhoeffer

"He gave up His life because He willed it, when He willed it, and as he willed it."
— St. Augustine of Hippo

"Christus suffered the extreme penalty during the reign of Tiberius at the hands of one of our procurators, Pontius Pilatus."
—Cornelius Tacitus, Roman historian

"My enemies surround me like a pack of dogs
   an evil gang closes in on me.
      They have pierced my hands and feet.
   I can count every bone in my body.
      My enemies stare at me and gloat.
   They divide my clothes among themselves
      and throw dice for my garments."

— Psalm 22:16-18, NLT

"Jesus hath many lovers of His heavenly kingdom, but few bearers of His Cross. He hath many seekers of comfort, but few of tribulation. He findeth many companions of His table, but few of His fasting. All desire to rejoice with Him, few are willing to undergo anything for His sake. Many follow Jesus that they may eat of His loaves, but few that they may drink of the cup of His passion. Many are astonished at His miracles, few follow after the shame of His Cross."

—Thomas à Kempis

"Let us who are the children of pain be now a bridge of reconciliation."
— St. Martin de Porres

"Father, into your hands
I commit my spirit."
—Luke 23:46, NIV

"Even on a cross, Jesus died like a child falling asleep in his father's arms."
—William Barclay

Sanctuary features the art of Troy Nilsson, a Christian artist, film composer and songwriter. He resides with his wife in Franklin, Tennessee. His art is featured on the cover, pages 2-3, 26-27, 49, 54-55, 74, 102-103, and 112-113 of this journal.

To see more of his artwork, visit www.nilssonmedia.org/troy.htm.